Short Vowel Phonics 2: short o, u, e

by: Patricia J. Norton

illustrated by: Sarah E. Cashman

Other reading material by the Author:

Short Vowel Phonics 1
Short Vowel Phonics 2, short a, i
Short Vowel Phonics 3
Short Vowel Phonics 4
Short Vowel Phonics 5
Short Vowel Phonics 6
Short Vowel Phonics Short Stories
Decodable Alphabet Chart

The story "Bugs and Bats" is dedicated to Emily and Jeff and the bats in their attic. Thanks to your bats, it was easier to enjoy the front porches in our neighborhood that summer.

ISBN: 978-0-9817710-2-1 (lib. bdg.)
[1. Reading - Phonetic method. 2. Reading readiness. 3. Phonics]

2nd printing

©2006 Patricia J. Norton
Illustrated by Sarah E. Cashman

shortvowelphonics.com

Manufactured in the U. S. A.

Text font: Pen Time Manuscript

Table of Contents

Short o Stories

Short u Stories

Short e Stories

The Hot Rod

Note to parents and teachers: Please have the child read the title before beginning the story. The title of the story, the pictures and the text are coordinated in such a way that a child will have read the word once before he or she is shown a picture of the word. This is to insure the child is learning to decode the word and not just guess.

Tod is a tot.

Tod is Bob's tot.

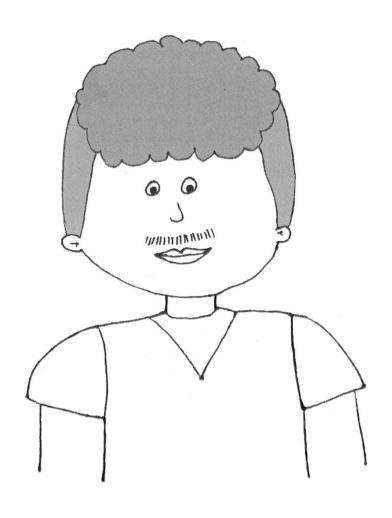

Bob has a top job.

Bob is a cop.

Bob is a pop and a cop.

Bob and Tod got a hot rod.

Bob and Tod had the top

hot rod on the lot.

Ron and Ron's Dog

Ron has a dog.

Dot is a dog.

Dot is Ron's dog.

Ron and Dot jog.

Ron and Dot jog on a bog.

The bog has a log.

Ron is hot. Dot is hot.

Ron and Dot hop on the log.

A fox and a hog hop on
the log.
Ron and Dot jog and jog
and jog.

A Fox and a Frog

A fox and a frog romp on

a bog.

The frog hops. The fox plods.

The frog and the fox spot

a pond.

The pond has a log.

The frog hops on the log.

The fox plops on the bog.

16

The frog has a top spot on
the log.

The fox has a top spot on
the bog.

Bud the Pup

Bud is a pup.

Bud dug in the mud.

Bud runs in the mud.

Bud runs and runs.

Mud is fun.

But mud on Bud bugs Mum.

Mum: "Cut the fun. Up in

the tub, Bud."

Is the tub fun?

Bugs and Bats

Bugs bug Gus.

But bats sup on bugs.

Mom and Pop Bat sup on

big bugs.

Yum, Yum!

Mom and Pop Bat had six

pups: Pug, Pun, Pup, Jug-Jug,

Zug, and Tux.

And bat kids sup on bugs.
At the Bat's hut, bugs can
not bug Gus.

A Cub's Grub

Tut is a cub.

Tut is snug in a hut.

Tut is as snug as a bug in

a rug.

Up jumps Tut.

Tut must sup.

Tut hunts grubs.

Scum is on the grubs.

Yuck!

Tut hunts nuts.

Yum!

The cub hunts plums.

Tut scrubs the plums.

Tut sups in the sun.

Yum, a plump plum!

The Red Hen

Peg is a pet red hen.

The hen had a pen.

Lek fed the hen.

Lek set Peg in the den.

The hen met Ted.

Lek let Ted pet the hen.

The end.

A Wren and a Sled

Glen is a wren.

Glen has a nest.

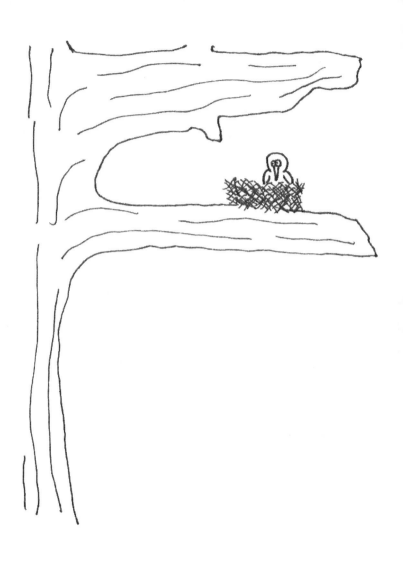

Glen's nest is the best nest.

Meg had a sled.

Meg sped on the sled.

Glen met Meg.

Meg and Glen sped on
the sled.

At the bend, Meg sped left.

Glen fled west.

Glen slept in the nest.

In a bed, Meg had a rest.

The Sick Hen

Lek's hen, Peg, sat in the pen.

Peg got sick.
The hen had a red neck.

Lek: "A vet can fix Peg."

Lek and Peg went in a quick
cab.

Lek begs the vet, "Fix Peg."

The vet sets a hot pack on
the hen's neck.

The vet and the hot pack fix
Peg's neck.

Back in the pen, Peg pecks.

And Lek sits in his den.